Escaping Mental Illness:
Challenges Towards Triumph

By: Denise Broadway

Wade Christian Publishing

EPHESIANS 2:10

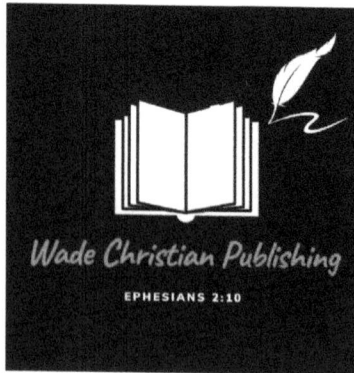

Escaping Mental Illness:
Challenges Towards Triumph

Written by Denise Broadway

ISBN: 979-8-9914674-0-7

Wade Christian Publishing LLC
www.wadepublishers.com
info@wadepublishers.com

Dedications

In memory of my parents, Bernard and Virginia Broadway

I dedicate my achievements to you. Thank you for your loving support and welcoming me as your daughter. My accomplishments are a representation of your dedicated devotion to me. Thank you for guiding my Spiritual Surviving Journey. HE knows, we are leading our family's obtainable Wealth on Earth and ABOVE.

Your loving daughter, Niecie

A Family's Wealth on Earth and ABOVE

A family that Prays together will have a fulfilled life,

for all the children, husband, and wife.

Family must keep all ties,

that will not be broken by deceit or lies.

We have a Heritage and Legacy on this land.

Our lives are either accepted or rejected,

awaiting OUR FATHER'S HAND.

This is the life to release, relax, and rejoice.

It is up to your decisions

and structures to make a choice.

We are crying out for forgiveness.

 Our strength will control the weakness.

We must keep a path for our children to lead

and help them with the will to succeed.

OUR FATHER will give us ETERNAL LIFE.

We must distinguish between who lies below

and WHOM you should love.

We await HIS Arrival

in hopes that JESUS will Bless

a Family's Wealth on Earth and ABOVE.

To My Children and Grandchildren

I am 65 years old and have 2 children,

10 grandchildren, and 3 great-grandchildren.

It may be true and clear to see

there could be more grands to fulfill the tree.

If this journey I've taken is fulfilling,

I'm taking it to the highest hill.

It's been said: "The Apple Doesn't Fall Far from The Tree."

Looking in the mirror, it is not hard to see,

you all have the seed that came from me.

Remember and acknowledge to another,

there is no one to replace your mother.

When searching and receiving,

you've got to find the missing link,

just take the time to Pray and think.

I constantly Pray that every day

my love, respect, and guidance flow your way,

so don't go astray, for the Calling is near to stay.

It has always been my life's hopes and dreams

that you all find love here on Earth and finally ABOVE.

I don't take kindness for weakness, always take a stand.

When I leave this land, you are on cue,

it's time to reach for that OPEN HAND.

FATHER GOD I hope when they are guided to receive

ETERNAL Love and Happiness,

they see and distinguish all there is to understand.

Love, Mom

To My FATHER ABOVE and My Dad

HEAVENLY FATHER, I thank You for

 the Strength and Knowledge You've given me.

I yearn for wisdom and prosperity.

You fulfill me with an abundance of blessings,

until one's final resting.

Devotion and Dedication to Your name,

it's known to be compelling to feel the same.

FATHER from ABOVE,

YOU are my only first love!

My life is determined for

the proposal I'm praying of.

My Dad on Earth,

you have walked with me

down the lane to commitment

for the first time.

Oh, was I so blind!

This wasn't a blast!

So, there's stones to cast.

Finally, I understand

and I'm completely aware of

distinguishing between a boy and a man.

My calling is blissfully falling; it's on cue,

and the blessings are far from stalling.

Compassion paired with wisdom

and trust is a must.

In the path of nurturing,

Love is dedicated to

"My FATHER ABOVE" and My Dad.

I'll always love you!"

November 10th, 1934 - July 31st, 2007

(Bernard Broadway)

The Love She Thought I Never Had

She is all the woman, I shared a life to understand,

for the dilemmas and distractions swayed at hand.

I know there were times of worries and frustrations,

but the happy moments will forever out way

the person I portray.

You are a strong gifted woman to be married for 50 years.

The fears and tears have surely bestowed the rears,

keeping your love, which, we see, is so incredibly dear.

I hope and pray having my second marriage

will embrace and give me strength,

tolerance, and your courage.

There is always a walk the walk

and talk the talk,

but seeing you travel, with Destiny,

has shown to be,

and you have acknowledged that fate,

has proclaimed guidance and acceptance

with your appointed mate.

The dedication for all the love,

listening and learning you set before me,

9

it is compelling to be,

what you have set out to see.

Now, say to your mother,

there will never be another

to lead me further,

for honesty and trust

is always to be nurtured.

I feel blessed and enriched

for there are no doubts

to be enforced or left unsaid,

because my mother will always know:

The Love She Thought I Never Had!!!!

February 8th,1937 - August 19th, 2014 (Virginia Broadway)

My Daughter's Influence is Always a Great Part of My Life

Raising you as my first child and daughter,

I was so young, having a one-of-a-kind,

newly delightful experience.

As a new mother, I saw early,

your growing potential

and unique qualities surface very abruptly.

It was expressed and portrayed to vision:

My Daughter as I See Me.

The focus was encountered, released, and fulfilled,

with the Blessings of our 4th Generation of Women.

The lives of our grandchildren

will be dedicated to this upcoming world,

as their journey to depend and comprehend

as resilient growing children.

Having the will to achieve,

our walk is in HIS PATH, ours to BELIEVE.

You're now a woman holding your own,

always consistent, and travels close to home.

The love is so nurturing; never feel alone.

We are so thankful for the usage of the cell phone.

You are a special woman I admire,

for all your challenges given

and your will to seek.

The upholding and the rescues,

I feel are so very beholding.

HIS OBSERVATION

is for my determination and sacrifices.

Your recognition will be rewarded

for your daily dedication.

I thank you dearly for your support,

with great appreciation.

Keeping the focus intact, It's a fact,

It's relevant for my encouragement,

it's with requirement and acknowledgment:

My Daughter's Influence is Always a Great Part of My Life.

To My Loving Son

There's no question or doubt,

I deliver My love as a Mother.

You are my son, and in life's challenges,

you'll take chances as "A Man Taking a Stand!"

You will release my hand!

Give with your love

the guidance of your children.

The nurturing they need is to succeed!

Let's rely on the will to Pray,

with the love of HIS PROTECTION.

Pray, and stay focused!

There is a Calling from OUR LORD, ABOVE.

I'm seeing, every possibility

of a motivating man excelling his capabilities!

There are steps to follow as an admirable modest

and aggressive man, staying firm in your responsibilities.

Take note: Aim high!

Reach, toward the sky!

There's no limit!

You'll always try,

keep your head afloat!

A man should always take heed

in wearing his raincoat!

Becoming a man,

there's a new discovery ahead!

The chance of accepting or denial,

the recovery will lead!

Remember: I'm your mother!

Walking together, a family as one,

has the ability to hear the Word, HE will Feed.

We will recover every challenge,

our step for Glory to proceed.

Our hearts will open and look toward ETERNITY.

A Mother and Son's Eternal Love

has a life's message to be accounted for and heard.

There is no question or doubt:

I Deliver My Love as Your Mother.

Never Forget

GOD will open another doorway to recovery,

with a transition conquered and delivered as an eye opener,

also the Blessings of not a closure saying Goodbye.

It is just a blink of the eye

obtained when seeking direction

toward the gates of DESTINY.

Holding tight to HIS HAND

is always a must for survival of the heart's impurities

rendered with SALVATION

to be covered in a SPIRITUAL WALK.

FAITH and DEVOTION are honored

with daily WORSHIP for OUR FATHER.

There is one KING TO SERVE and OBEY

for the respect of Acceptance with the love of HIS NAME.

Keep your head held high

with no unstructured complications

to rekindle any unsure possibilities of stepping backward

toward an unlikely placement to fulfill a breakdown

or the non-survival of His strongholds

of Mental Illness in the makings.

Learning to accept and reject

when needed is your call of sanity

or a strong grip to recovery.

Table of Contents

Introduction

Mental illness has affected over 450,000,000 people worldwide with some sort of condition. It has been known to dominate and control the mind into feeling lifeless and powerless. Mental illness is awaiting a healthy takeover! Mr. Mental Illness, as I call it, can relate to the lives of many people. It's been a mind-power seed, rooting weakness, shortcomings, and struggles into one's mind. It can make you feel helpless and weak. But, you can obtain a reachable reality by learning to have an exceptional outlook toward an exclusive, therapeutic guide. Claiming your strength and resilience can be fully rewarding!

Don't Give Up! Be mindful and alert when making decisions to overpower any emptiness! Keep fulfilling, conquering, and exceeding all your goals and aspirations!! Always remember to put God first to guide your journey towards a fruitful "Destination"!!!

Say the following affirmations to strengthen your mind:

- Walks of struggles lead to many hurdles in my life that I'm able to see!!!
- There are open doors that never closed on me!!!
- Chances were my advances!!!
- The lengthy barriers of Mr. Mental Illness, have given me extraordinary strength to overcome the season!!!!
- I am a Mental Illness Survivor, Pledging Our Love as One People!
- I have overcome Mental Illness and am Learning to Live with Life's Limitations!

1: The Talk They Never Mention (Mental Illness)

Mental Illness, as I experienced, is a journey all of its own. To live it is to talk about it. I never actually read materials or pamphlets per say. I lived it and am still recovering. There is now an exceptional amount of Literature about Mental Illness, but not back in the day. I first encountered the illness as a teenager. Back then, everybody thought that when you had a breakdown, you were crazy and to keep it Hush Hush in the family. Most people don't understand and feel if you have an illness, you might hurt them or yourself, especially when it hits and controls you. I've known it to be a fact with myself and others related to me. There is a certain time of year when this illness tries or succeeds to take over your body and mind and leaves you powerless. Mental Illness has been around for hundreds of years. But for 44 yrs, I've been trying to, as they say: "Put a handle on it," and so far, I have it at a point where I'm in control.

Every time "Mr. Mental Illness" tries to take over, there is an out-and-out war between me and it. All I can say is, it has been the ride of a lifetime, and trying to level out the right medicine to sustain you is a journey all of its own. Let me say this: Talk to someone, a family member, friend, teacher, Priest, or anybody you feel comfortable with when you feel depressed, paranoid, lonely, lifeless, extra lazy, no desire for sex, no passion for life, and having everything bottled inside. Please release those feelings by relating to someone else who you feel will understand and seek help for you or whomever the troubled one may be.

2: We Are Human Too

Guess what? We love, we care, we sing, we dance, and we need your help to understand. Just a few words to say: 10 fingers, 10 toes, and every part of the body you were born with, we have been Blessed with too. Crying, Laughing, and reaching out is what everybody has encountered throughout their life.

Relationships are the highest point in one's life. We fall in and out of love, have children, relate or cope with everyday past, present, and future endeavors. You know what? We give you chances, so why can't you return the favor?

GOD has a plan for everyone. How you deal with your hand will determine where you land. Sometimes, we take similar roads and end up in the same place, but we are all human, and life is a trip for anyone.

3: Testimonies To Tell It All

As I said before, 18 was a troubled age, and everything was handled so exceptionally differently in 1975. I was married, pregnant with a child, and started my first real job. When those several years of turmoil and frustration rolled in at the age of 21, I rolled out. Unknowingly, "Mr. Mental Illness" was around the corner. I never let on I was suffering as a new mother with Life's Limitations. I can honestly say from the age of 21 to 30 was the life of a lifetime. When that time of year came around to visit, "Ms. Bi-Polar" was all she wrote.

Visiting several Institutions and hospitals, it was evident I had a serious problem. When I moved to Georgia in 1989, it was a new life and time to reinforce any and all pathways in my life being for or against me. This was the land where I was going to make a stand. It's been years since I last visited the power and convictions of "Mr. Mental Illness" to take over and place me in the hospital to experiment with me. Realizing I could cope and be stabilized at the same time, this was going to be the answer.

Please listen, talk, and possibly teach another about the seriousness and capabilities of letting it hit you again and again and control the outcome. Believe me, you can be in control, at least if you take therapy sessions, medication, or both. "Mr. Mental Illness" wants you to feel there is no way out and you can't talk it out.

Remember This: Read a Scripture from The Bible, then Pray before and after over the problem, turn it over to GOD, and Let It Go!!!!!

4: Caring, Caught Up, and Can Now Let Go

Since the age of 27, I cared and was caught up for 21 years. What was it going to take to Let Go and move on? Procrastination, cheap talk, and a loose tongue led this ride to the ride of all times. Meeting new friends or companions was a true treat, but "Mr. Party All the Time", never saw more than a casual good time. "Mr. Party All the Time" always blocked those new Blessings and kept me lingering onto a dream, but he never prevailed.

Now was the time to live and go with the flow, or never look back and Let it Go!!! I chose to stop making U-turns, Short Cuts, and Playing in the Danger Zone. In the past, "Mr. Party All the Time", was a blast, but we both knew it would never last. I hope you find what you're looking for because GOD has opened a Door that has given me so much more.

5: You Can Cope Too

Adapting to an illness is like smoking a cigarette. After all the medicine is administered or time to put the butt out, you still have the yearning or desire to want or need more. Explain your need to talk with Doctors, Nurses, Teachers, Counselors, Family Members, Friends, and Priests. Many more outlets we're looking to Release, Relate, and Demonstrate. You need to acknowledge the differences and understand what is self-motivating, what is the same, and what doesn't make you feel less worthy.

This illness is HEREDITARY and can stem from hundreds of years ago. It is a trait that can proclaim you or any descendant. I feel this illness is as deadly as Cancer. It may be the disease of all time; this is just my observation.

Try this: Cope, Cuddle Daily, Calm Down, Catch a breath, and Continue to LET GOD lead your Destiny. You're going to be on the Highest and most profound Hill, so just Listen and Take Your Pill.

6: You Can Fight It, But Don't Lose It

Listen when I tell you, it is all an upsweep ride to a whole new life; one to Gain, Gather, and Grab. Good people are hard to find, but when you meet them, you want to keep them and continue enjoying to know them. This disease has been a battle for men, women, and children. We can fight together, but don't end it in turmoil. If you know the 4 W's, you have almost won the battle to succeed.

1. Wait: Listen, Release, Let Go!

2. Watch Out: There is always a hater; time to say: " I Feel You Later"

3. Weather the Storm: Always strive for the best and let all obstacles stay at rest!

4. Win and Retrieve: All Life's pitfalls and take Glory to the finish.

   It is time for healing; all things can happen and become possible through CHRIST.

7: Live, Love, and Let Go

Live life to the fullest. You've got only one lifetime to share and be happy. You have so much to live for. A happy life is the Cure for any and every disease as long as your Faith overrides your weaknesses. Loving GOD first, yourself, your better half, and your children will all fall in place without a doubting trace. Love is like a weapon; it has all the capabilities to hurt you or anyone else. Love, Laughter, and Living Life to the fullest is the largest legacy to keep you on your P's and Q's. Now you can finally Let Go!

8: Life, Sex, and a Misunderstanding

Life, as I see it, is full of challenges. There is only one life you live, and when it's time to close the book, That's it! It's always been my hopes and dreams that I find love here on Earth and finally ABOVE. When you have finally met that special someone, it is the beginning of life shared that you will never forget. Sex is like the memories we shared last night; it was clear to me, all was brought to light, if I may, should I say: This Love Feels Right!!!!! Having Sex is time, Fulfillment, Love, and a tune-up every oil change I need.

9: Passion, Poetry, and Peace of Mind

Jesus is the head of my household. Know it's been a
struggle filled with negative releases,
but, HE's always there to sweep, brush through,
and pick up the pieces.

Yet hungry, Grace is leading us to a fulfilling
and sustaining PLACE.
HE knows when it's time to reach toward
the opening of the approachable lock
and the closure of the timeless clock.
Let's follow HIM to the PEARLY GATES
where all awaits the joining FLOCK.
Sleepless nights are full of dreams
leading to the awakening lights.
 If you've accomplished the need to succeed,
then, I know it's relevant, for HE
is the knowledge you're hungry to feed.

Our FATHER "GOD", will conquer, destroy,

and restructure this forbidden land.

We have stumbled, fallen, and now standing.

To reframe from the downfalls, upsweeps, and crossfires,

our HEARTS are constantly shifting,

and SOULS are now uplifting.

Thank you, DEAR JESUS,

for everything YOU put before and beside me.

Let's keep the Devil behind

and unapproachable to never abide.

This evil spirit you find

is the only one of its kind.

Demons lead a destiny to reframe

from a life full of Spiritual Fame.

Let's never accept or claim to believe to foresee,

just say repeatedly the Devil will forever flee.

Now, I ask you without a doubt,

the abundance enforce,

is your designated choice.

Let's rejoice,

and give HIM the PRAISE!

HIS Angels will generate the journey

and keep us amazed.

We're uplifting our voices,

crying for deliverance,

and accepting the past,

present, and future choices.

HE stands in the SAND.

We reach out for HIS HAND,

understanding and acknowledging,

how JESUS sacrificed all sins on this forsaken land.

When you find you may fall behind,

keep in mind, "GOD" knows -- IT'S TIME TO LET GO,

AND LET "GOD"

10: There Is No Walk With the Devil

When I lay to sleep at night,

I pray to awaken another BLESSED daylight.

Every day, I look ABOVE and say: We love You, FATHER GOD.

Thank You, FATHER GOD, for our vision to see

and the whispers we hear so loud, yet softly clear.

We are BLESSED to speak and talk,

with the rhythm of stepping in stride

as we crawl to walk.

With all our BLESSINGS that come our way,

we PRAY and convey, hoping to live and see that

EVERLASTING PROMISED DAY.

As we touch and feel,

there's also an anointing reaching, toward ABOVE,

yearning for only HIS LOVE.

There's GLORY to uphold

and Fear to withhold,

for a negative light is a must not

to travel a journey young or old.

This message is never to unfold!!!!

The testimonies we deliver and share

are one's will to care,

never to judge, for this isn't your call,

It's HIS, if you dare!!!

Growing, nurturing, loving,

and becoming a deserving Being,

bestow your FAITH, with commitment for DELIVERANCE,

because HE is knowing and seeing,

deciding one's choice for freeing!!!!!

You have nothing to offer this world.

We were told of you since early years as a boy or girl.

Never your will in gear.

You won't see our time for you in any year.

We won't Listen from your burning ear!!!

Devil, you will take your final fall.

HIS FORGIVENESS is your walk

for the possible FREEDOM HALL.

Make your plea, Our GOD will let you stand,

hopefully promise to us all!!!!

It's your choice!!!!!

When trying to flee or backslide,

It's time to PRAY and voice,

just stand to reach for HIS HAND

only to climb tall

for only our GOD to CALL.

Everyone must acknowledge, voicing to talk,

there is no walk and level with Mr. Devil.

11: All About Children

God has given us a gift to love, nurture, and become the best parents a child can dream of. They want love and happiness, and we can give them joy, comfort, clothing, and food to provide at our best.

It's a must! It's up to us!
Let's provide a home and all the packages a child will want, and we won't give them a complaint or reason to fuss.
They say men and women come a dime a dozen,
but children come a gift from Heaven!
Some have a special need. Some grow to fully succeed.
Some want you to listen, cope, and sit back as they read.
Some don't ever find a home for the nourishment you can provide to love or feed. They give you their joy, hope, love, and encouragement to advance and succeed.

Give them the right road to lead. Now, let's say once again, so everyone can comprehend...
Children love what you can give and what they can send.
It's not all about you!!!!

Remember, it's all about the children.

When it's time for another year to come and go,

this will be a covenant with JESUS,

WHOM we love and know!

Don't take Life for granted,

your Blessings will come, don't rush.

Only HE knows the Blessings of abundance

and the necessities that's a must!

In your Destiny, as you reach HIS KINGDOM,

there will be no more confessions or confusion.

12: More Blessings To Come

Be in Prayer for what you want.

Be Blessed for what you need.

Be thankful for what you receive.

We know and accept that JESUS

is the ONLY ONE to BELIEVE.

Let's Pray at night

to awaken to another daylight.

The struggles and triumphs

are destined to ride through the bumps,

shaky grounds, hurdles, and humps.

As you Pray to feast on this special day,

remember the bread and drink

are the first nourishment to be thankful in every way.

On HIS BIRTHDAY, let's rejoice

and have time to share, give, and praise,

for we know how HE had RAISED.

WE THANK YOU FOR EVERYTHING!

During the holidays, festive occasions, and the new year ahead, we give thanks to Him for everything. His love and protection are all the thanks he could ever bring.

Thank You:

For all You do for me

For the eyes to see

The voice to speak and the noise to hear

Courage and the will not to fear

Strength of walking and talking

A peaceful sleep and an awakening bright morning

The love, compassion, and consideration you bring

knowledge to learn

Wisdom and prosperity I'll earn

For the love You show

The protection from things I don't know

Thank You for being all things to us:

a mother, father, counselor, physician,

provider, protector, husband, and wife.

These are just a few to discuss Your position in our life.

Thank You for reaching out Your hands

for everyone's journey toward the Promise Land.

As we hear, walk, talk, and some sing,

Father God, we thank You for everything!

13: A Mother and Son's Eternal Love

My loving son, I cherish the day you keep abreast,

when all has failed, and you won't bail.

There is no other like your mother!

In this life, it reflects from me, for any concerning wife.

You've got to find that missing link,

just take the time to pray and think.

I know it's hard to keep the power and sanity of a man.

I don't take kindness for weakness; I always take a stand.

When I leave this land,

you're on cue, it's time to be a man.

I constantly pray that every day

my love, respect, and guidance, flow your way,

so, please don't go astray, for the calling is near to stay.

FATHER GOD, you held my hand,

for guiding this man, to reach out and understand.

We will always look above to honor,

"A mother and son's eternal love."

14: My Grand-Children, The Seeds From Within

Every night I lay peacefully praying

to open my eyes

and have the light shine from ABOVE

to cherish all of you

and find that you have my unconditional love.

The memories never fade, for your hand

has reached the limit to know and understand,

THIS MAN was sacrificed for our sins on this land!!

My Grand-Children are a part of me that I see only,

to acknowledge and never time or chance to feel lonely.

What will it take to give back to find,

the missing treasures that were left behind?

Knowing where your roots fall is the biggest journey of all.

I love you all as you may sometimes in life fall,

but try your best to live and ride through the big haul.

So, let's try this together throughout the stormy roads

and let THE LORD guide your road test,

reaching the heights to never second guess!!

Now I can say and always depend,

on My Grand-Children, The Seeds from Within.

15: My Daughter As I See Me

I was only 18 when we met,

the beginning of life and never to forget.

You and I have a bond to relate

and when time shows no fate.

We bring love and strength throughout the trait.

Now, it's time to bring your knowledge to the plate,

without consistency, the journey is too late.

It's been said "The apple doesn't fall far the tree."

Looking in the mirror it's not hard to see,

you have the seed that came from me.

You have grown to be quite a special woman

that any man would give his open hand.

Learning and accepting your need to succeed,

it's evident you're a definite catch indeed.

Now you have your daughters to proclaim their fate,

scheduling the date for their mate,

bringing to suffice their wedding day for the falling rice.

Remember and acknowledge to another

there is no one to replace mother.

It has always been my life's hopes and dreams

that we find love here on Earth and finally ABOVE.

I respect and cherish our nurturing heart to never depart.

Now we're free to see

"My Daughter As I See Me"

"YOU'RE NOW A WOMAN"

They say children are a gift from heaven!

I say you are special and one of many Christian women.

Now that you will finally leave the nest,

you will be full of ideas, dreams,

And become the woman with capabilities at your best.

Being a woman, you must stand tall,

not letting your emotions fall,

And let Jesus lead you to a ride to eternity

for a Worship wake-up call.

This has been a learning tool!

You have completed high school!

Your stepping stone to college shows

you have smarts because you are nobody's fool!

Remember, friends can be passive or strong.

Passing judgment is wrong!

Friends don't put on a hate mode.

Only an enemy shares this forsaken road.

One day when you settle down to a blessed marriage,

He will send that perfect guy to endure your strength,

tolerance, and courage.

You're no longer a girl to be unaccounted for in this world.

It's now time to unleash and hold tight to His hand!

Learn all you can, make a plan,

don't get sidetracked by a man!

Stay focused, "You're now a woman."

16: Take A Stand, You're A Man Now

When you finally left the nest, you became a man
full of ideas, dreams, and capabilities at your best.
I know it's been a struggle of a battle worth the fight.
The way you became a full-strength man was everything
you did wrong, but finally made attempts to fly right.
All the encounters of unforgettable nights
brought fears to tears for forgiveness, hoping to see
breakthroughs throughout the awakening daylight.
You continued tussling, fighting, and aggressing the anger
with all your might. Now that you have the journey intact,
keep your composure, knowing just how to act. Please
keep it enforced. You have made the perfect decision, I'm
glad you made this choice.
I hope your destination is at a level of completion,
and there will be no back tracks to lead to deception.
I love what I'm seeing, you're everything a woman is
hoping her man is being.
You are available and hoping for the courage,
to find that perfect woman to love
and settle down to a Blessed marriage.

OUR FATHER from ABOVE

has given and sent these words of encouragement:

LET GO OF MY HAND!

TAKE A STAND!

YOU'RE NOW A MAN!!!

17: What Is CAR

W-hich road will I take for the love I always forsake?

H-is body is fierce and always keeps a deep shine.

A-fter all, we chose this path because we lived on it so long as the miles progressed.

T-his is it! You're the right size, and there's always room for more.

I-love you for five more years or mileage, whatever comes first.

S-top and think out loud: is this worth the price?

C-ountless nights go by, and I wonder if I will make it home tonight?

A-ll I ask of you is time, fulfillment, love, and a tune-up every oil change I need.

R- ight now you don't owe me anything. All I ask is that you last one more night.

18: My New Love

M---ake this day never go away, for the feelings in my heart are never geared to depart.

Y---ou are a true Blessing, I Prayed to fulfill, for I feel this Journey is on the highest hill.

N---ow it is time for us to put our love on the line and Pray for Endurance to the end of time.

E---ver you feel in doubt, remember it is sure to say "I'm Out."

W---hether this is surely true, guess what? I'm taking a chance on you.

L---et's follow this road together and see where it will land, I'm reaching out to an OPEN HAND.

O------pen the book of life and turn to the page where you see togetherness for ETERNAL LIFE.

V---- ictory we can share to the end, because Baby, there is no women or men that can cast a stone to keep us alone.

E ----verlasting love is what I Prayed ABOVE to acknowledge and find, Tell me are you "My New Love"?

19: Thank You GOD for The Many Blessings

I Stand with You, I've Finally Made It,

I've Achieved My Own!!!!! A Recovery of a Touch-down!

Made another overpass to tackle Mr. Tight-end.

He wants a field goal. We won the game again,

against The Devil's Underachievers.

We know WHO Always SCORES!

HE IS OUR QUARTER-BACK, OUR FATHER GOD.

HE'S OUR #1 OFFENSE OR DEFENSE PLAYER ON HIS COURT.

HE is OUR POINT GUARD! The Devil makes another foul!

He falls down court, trying to score. During HIS

RECOVERING Defense, OUR FATHER, Blocks another Brick!

HE is also OUR 3 POINTER.

1. He accepts or denies the request of Blessings.

2. HE IS OUR PROVIDER.

3. HE'S OUR #1 OFFENSE or DEFENSE PLAYER on HIS
   COURT.

HE STANDS AS the protector or THE destructor.

Let's hope HE won't become THE DETECTOR,

waiting as Your REJECTOR.

We are all Reflectors! He made a grand slam!

The Devil is hiding in left field.

When in motion to score, He strikes-out!

It's now time you RECEIVE the Pitch to BELIEVE!!

The Blessings are full and loaded.

HE decides if #1. The Praises,

or #2. The Dedication for Devotion

and #3. A Surviving Salvation are all Home Runs towards,

HIS RECOVERING GRAND SLAM!

He's Reaching and Crying Out for YOU.

I've prayed to lead him to you.

It was plain to see his love was clear to me.

We hope he's found that missing link,

just taking the time to Pray and think.

I will always be here to open my heart

and OUR FATHER will keep us near and never apart.

Don't you ever forget to call HIS NAME,

regardless who's at blame or shows no shame,

we Pray for Glory to know the difference

or acknowledge the same.

Remember me as I carried the seed

for the love and trust HE planted to fulfill your need.

HEAVENLY FATHER, THANK YOU for releasing him

and keeping him close and near,

to follow YOU and never fear to hear

I know his heart is dear.

Just say it every night and know it's right

I love YOU LORD MY SAVIOR

I now feel He's Reaching and Crying Out for YOU.

Thank you, Father God, for my knowledge to write,

and an ability to express my journey with others.

I'll keep looking forward! I won't Judge!

I'll let GOD guide my Quest.

I'll rebuke The Devil from His final request.

This is my dedication toward a Spiritual Surviving Test.

I have learned and accepted that being in control of my emotions and actions (a must) makes life much healthier and fulfilling. Thank you, FATHER, for a new journey that's more satisfying, self-motivating, and a complete steady outreach towards a desired fruitful destiny.

Milton Keynes UK
Ingram Content Group UK Ltd.
UKHW020711251124
451531UK00018B/207